Two Plays

Niyi Osundare

UNIVERSITY PRESS PLC.
IBADAN
2005

University Press PLC
IBADAN ABA ABUJA AJEGUNLE AKURE BENIN IKEJA
ILORIN JOS KADUNA KANO MAKURDI ONITSHA
OWERRI WARRI ZARIA.

© Niyi Osundare 2005

ISBN 978 030 568 8
ISBN-13: 978-978-030-568-0

Published by University Press PLC
Three Crowns Building, Jericho, P.M.B. 5095, Ibadan, Nigeria
Fax: 02-2412056   E-mail: unipress@stannet.com
Website: www.universitypressplc.com

The Author

Educated at the Universities of Ibadan, Leeds and York (Toronto), Niyi Osundare is the author of over twelve volumes of poetry, four plays, and numerous essays and articles on African literature and culture. A believer in poetry as performance, he has performed his poetry in different parts of the world, and his poems have been translated into French, Dutch, Czech, Slovenia, German, Italian, and Korean.

Osundare has won many national and international prizes, including the Association of Nigerian Authors (ANA) Poetry Prize, The ANA/Cadbury Poetry Prize, the Commonwealth Poetry Prize, and the Noma Award, Africa's most prestigious Book Award. In 1998 he was the recipient of the Fonlon/Nichols Award for "excellence in literary creativity combined with significant contributions to Human Rights in Africa". He has also received honorary doctorates from Universite de Toulouse-Le Mirail in Franklin Pierce College in New Hampshire, USA.

For the past three decades, Osundare has been a provocative contributor to public discourse on culture, politics and the economy. Nigeria remains his area of focus, though the umbrella of his concern covers the African continent and the world at large. At the centre of this concern are issues such as human rights, social justice, and the environment, which he has pursued with characteristic perspicacity and passion.

A former Professor of English, University of Ibadan, Nigeria, he is now a Professor of English, University of New Orleans, U. S. A.

THE MAN WHO WALKED AWAY

CHARACTERS

DÈYÍ	-	A middle-aged, medium-sized man who works as a machine operator at Pantibury Overseas Limited.
ÀBẸ̀KẸ́	-	His wife. A strikingly beautiful woman in her early thirties.
TÓYÌN	-	Their daughter, aged about twelve.
SỌLÁ	-	Their son, aged about nine.
ÌYÁ ÀGBÀ		A tall and overbearing woman in her fifties.
LANDLORD		A short Shylock-like figure.
GÒKÈ} AKIN }	-	Both friends to Dèyí
RICH MAN		A short and rather corpulent man.
BAR-MAID		The Rich man's Retinue including his two courtesans. A Music Band.

I

A sitting room with two entrances. The right entrance is covered with a faded, over-used door curtain; the left is simply left open. To the top of the curtained entrance hangs something which looks like the national flag of a country. In the centre of the back wall is hung a cardboard chart on which the following is boldly printed:
MOTTO: **WHEN THEIR'S LIFE, THEIR'S HOPE.**

On the right side of the room is a rickety couch so worn out that the inside foam peeps out in several places. Against the left wall leans an old bicycle with the front wheel and tyre removed and the rear tyre in an advanced stage of puncture.

The lights gradually reveal a woman in the front centre of the room, literally perched on a creaking chair, monologuing to an ancient manual sewing machine on a table before her. The machine rattles on.

ÀBÉKÉ: You even don't need to complain so noisily. I know you are old and need an *aburo (Younger brother or sister)*. Like an old man with a toothless gum you now swallow those things you used to chew. But chew or swallow, you will sew this small piece for me.

(Tries the hand wheel, and it jams). I know you do more skipping than sewing but you will surely sew this for me. Yes, you will. Last week I asked my friend at Dugbe to mend a little hole in Toyin's gown and she asked me to pay fifty naira. 'Fifty naira', I exclaimed. 'E e', she replied. 'Since the government people brought *Udoji* the small money we have has melted in our hands. The elephant's greed has made the forest a starving region for rodents.

Sews a little bit, then pauses to readjust the wheel. That's one thing about my friend the seamstress. She sews words as well as clothes. *Lọ́rọ̀ kan ṣá, (in brief),* I brought home Toyin's gown to do it myself. Just look at it: I bought this gown *(Spreads it out to the audience)* for twenty naira from the *bosikona* people; now I am being asked to mend it for fifty naira. If I were that rich, I would not be living in this rat hole. *(Surveys the room).* I would have been living at Bodija, Kongi, U.I. *(Pronounced Yu Hai)* with servants tending my flower beds, washing my dirty clothes, cleaning my shoes, walking my dog in the evenings, rocking my little ones to sleep.

The monologue is interrupted by a loud knock on the left door. Tóyìn and Ṣọlà run in.

TÓYÌN & ṢỌLÁ: *Ẹ kuu 'lé Mama* (Good day, Mama).
O o, ẹ káàbọ̀.(Welcome) How was school?

ÀBÈKÉ: Today is Friday. Didn't you bring your report cards?

TÒYÍN: I scored an 'A', Mama, and our teacher said it was the best in the class.

ÀBÈKÉ: Un un un Toyin, your score in Social Studies is not so good this time. Why?

TÒYÍN: The teacher asked how many people should sleep in one room and I answered nine: three on the bed, three under the bed, and three on the remaining part of the floor.

ÀBÈKÉ: Then what did your teacher say?

TÒYÍN: He said I was wrong, and my classmates laughed at me.

(Àbèké shakes her head meaningfully from left to right and right to left).

TÒYÍN: Mama, the teacher says I'll go on school bursary to college: the school will pay half of my fees and my parents the other half. He said that is what the school does for the brightest pupil each year.

ÀBÈKÉ: And what did you tell your teacher?

TÒYÍN: I said that I like the bursary, and that my dad will be able to pay the other half since he works for a big company... So next year, mama, Toyin will be in a college, *(Demonstrates as she speaks)* going about with those big books in my arms, with an Oxford Maths set, big exercise books with the name of my college written boldly on them, speaking English and French at social gatherings, wearing school uniforms. When I leave college, I will go to university and become a doctor or a lawyer, or an engineer.

(Toyin's prophetic rhapsody is broken by the sullen entry of her father. Dèyí creeps in like a clobbered boxer and literally collapses into the couch which rattles as if that were its last burden).

TÓYÌN & SỌLÁ: *E kaabọ dadi.* (*Welcome daddy*).
(Dèyí nods in response)

ÀBẸ̀KẸ́: *Ó yá*, Toyin and Sọlá, go to the backyard and play. *(They exit).*

Ábẹ́kẹ́ quickly perches on the edge of the couch, her hands on Dèyí's despondent shoulders.

What's the matter? Why do you look so tired? Are you sick? Was there an accident at your work place?

DÈYÍ: Yes there was an accident, and my job was crushed under the weight of the master's pen.

ÀBẸ̀KẸ́: What... What do you mean?

DÈYÍ: I am fired!

ÀBẸ̀KẸ́: No... No. How can? Didn't you tell them we have kids to support, rent to pay, medicines to...

DÈYÍ: Àbẹ̀kẹ́, our manager is as automatic and impersonal as the machines we operate. He said he had orders from the company's headquarters in London to fire us... or 'retrench' as he put it. They say our products are not doing well on the market and so they have to cut production down and cut us out.

ÀBẸ̀KẸ́: And you were just sent home like that?

DÈYÍ: Yes, a hundred and fifty of us, without notice, without sympathy: just told like school boys about to start a holiday: 'eh... don't come tomorrow! Alright?'

ÀBẹ̀Kẹ́: Didn't you tell them about your families?

DÈYÍ: They say they never signed any contract with our families. It is not their business whether you and your family eat grass like the cows at Sángo. Just come to work when you're needed, and when you're not, go back. I understand our most supreme manager, the *ògá pátápátá* in London, is unmarried.

ÀBẹ̀Kẹ́: This is a most terrible time for this to happen. Dèyí, *(Pause)* I am expecting a baby. *(Dèyí didn't say a word. He rests his chin on his left palm with the fingers clenched, the left elbow fixed on his left knee. He was one big bundle of reflection and sorrow).*

ÀBẹ̀Kẹ́: *(Now very importunate)* Speak, Dèyí, at least that is one source of joy for us.

DÈYÍ: Yes, in normal times this would be a joy, but an expectant wife to a jobless man is the sure symptom of an imminent failure. Every normal Ojo and Ajayi can sleep with a woman and make a baby, but it takes the real man to raise it. *(Pause).* But when did I become that fingerless leper that cannot carry his own baby?

(Dèyí breaks down and as Àbẹ̀kẹ́ consoles him, light fades out on both of them).

II

Same scene as before. Ábẹ́kẹ́ sits on the couch, half-heartedly knitting. Ṣọlá sits beside her, pretending to read the captions in a picture-book. Then, book half-closed on his lap, he turns to Ábẹ́kẹ́.

ṢỌLÁ: Mama, Bade said my dad has no job; that he is a lazy man.

ÀBẸ̀KẸ́: Who is Bade?

ṢỌLÁ: Don't you know him again? The son of Professor Adeku-Roberts. The one who came the other time and said our room was smelling.

ÀBẸ̀KẸ́: *(Rather impatiently)* Un-hun...?

ṢỌLÁ: He said we are rats and that our room is a hole; that we eat our *eba* without meat, that...

ÀBẸ̀KẸ́: You shut up! So you've been listening to gossip and all that.

ṢỌLÁ: *(Obviously not ready to be shut up)* Mama, why do the Apenas have three big cars and we have none?

ÀBẸ̀KẸ́: Because they are businessmen.

ṢỌLÁ: Why do they keep a big dog at their gate?

ÀBẸ̀KẸ́: Do they?

ṢỌLÁ: Yes, the big one that barks day and night... it bit a beggar the other time.

ÀBẸ́KẸ́: Oh, I see, it is to drive off thieves?

SỌLÁ: Mama, why don't we become businessmen and become rich and have many cars and live in a big house?

The arrival of Dèyí puts an end to the dialogue. Sọlá jumps off the couch and Dèyí takes his place. Dèyí's food is put on a small stool before him. He eats absent-mindedly).

ÀBẸ́KẸ́: Dèyí, you must eat now, or you will just starve. Remember for the past few days, you have always scratched the top of your food. Yesterday you were so wrapped up in thought that you even forgot to wash your hands. Why?

DÈYÍ: *Màá bínú Ábẹ́kẹ́.* (Forgive me, Ábẹ́kẹ́) It's because I have no appetite.

ÀBẸ́KẸ́: What happened to your appetite?

DÈYÍ: I lost it.

ÀBẸ́KẸ́: Then you must find it! If your company wants to kill you, will you help them by killing yourself? When life's drum sounds *pami! pami! pami! (Kill me, Kill me, Kill me)* should we not devise a softer way of dancing to it?

DÈYÍ: Yes, if you have control over your own legs. Since I lost my job, I have become the grass of the wind-valley, bent head-to-ground in whatever direction the wind blows.

ÀBẸ́KẸ́: Why do you talk as if the end of the world has come. Come on, Dèyí, *Olówóorí mi, (My boss, my master)* heavier rains have fallen and the

	ground has sucked up their water. Where is the manhood you often boast of?
DÈYÍ:	That manhood is gone; it evaporated the day I lost my job. My manhood was crushed under the might of the personnel manager's pen.
ÀBẸ̀KẸ́:	No, you are still a man, my man.
DÈYÍ:	Do you call him a man who packs his family in this hovel competing hard with rats and cockroaches? Do you call him a man who for several weeks has not produced a single housekeeping *kobo** for his family? Do you call him a man that whose daughter tops her class but cannot send her to college? Do you call him a man, that one who plies the labour offices everyday and the only offer he gets is a 'come tomorrow' order? Do you call him a man who cannot provide a single bar of soap for his family?

(The Landlord enters. A stocky, rather brusque man that stands five odd feet from the ground. He's clad in a sumptuous damask ṣọ́rọ́ and dànsíkí. He carries a big pipe which he never smokes. Surveys the room).

LANDLORD: What have you people been doing to these walls? Look at that *(Points)*. It costs a fortune to paint these walls but no sooner are they painted than they are smeared again. Why? Do you people use the wall as your dining table?

---

* 'Kobo' is the lowest unit of Nigerian currency.

ÀBẸ̀KẸ́: I'm sure you know when you're insulting your tenants, *Oga* Landlord; and besides the lord of the land shouldn't lie. These walls have not been painted for two years.

LANDLORD: Is that true?

ÀBẸ̀KẸ́: Of course, it is. How would you know when you never come to see the rats you have in your holes? Your caretaker never comes except on collection days. Our roof has been leaking for several months now. When we told your caretaker he said the leaks are roof-windows that will let us see the moon at night.

LANDLORD: O... kay ... (*Coughs*) o ... right.
I shall tell the caretaker to take note. Now, where is your rent for this month?

ÀBẸ̀KẸ́: When did you start doing that job for yourself?

LANDLORD: I thought you still had a caretaker?
The caretaker has been away for three weeks to celebrate the ... (*Has a hard time remembering*) ... the twenty- ... sixth anniversary of his father's funeral. That's just by the way, anyway. Where is our thing for this month - *ṣẹkẹndí alùwọnjọn wọnjọ lápò ṣojú ọmọ rèjerèje.**
Àbẹ́kẹ́ and Dèyí hold a brief tet-a-tet.

---

*The real stuff, the one that jingles in the pocket and gives the owner a smooth face.

ÀBẸ́KẸ́: We can't pay you this month becau...
LANDLORD: You can't what? *(Holding his right ear with his right hand and tilting his head towards Àbẹ́kẹ́ and Dèyí)*
ÀBẸ́KẸ́: I say we can't pay.
LANDLORD: You can say that again. You can say it a thousand times but while you do, just stretch out a clenched fist and open it to reveal my thing for this month. Simple. Two thousand naira.
ÀBẸ́KẸ́: Ọ̀gá Landlord, we cannot find your rent.
LANDLORD: O may be you've not searched long enough. Have you looked *(Points)* at the corners of your room, underneath your bed, at...
ÀBẸ́KẸ́: I am sorry but we...
LANDLORD: Let me have it quick and crisp. I'm a man of money, not words.
ÀBẸ́KẸ́: Please listen to me. We...
LANDLORD: I am a money man and my ears only respond to the sound of money: the jingling of coins, the rustling of notes.
ÀBẸ́KẸ́: So you don't even have an ear for the suffering of poor tenants.

The landlord fidgets with his pipe for some time, looks straight at Àbẹ́kẹ́, then Dèyí who sits all the time with his head drooping in his hands. The landlord suddenly turns serious and begins to harangue the couple.

LANDLORD: I can't find it, I can't find it. (*Pause*). 'I can't-find-it' is the disease of poor tenants. But the landlord's stubborness is its cure. You think you can just live here for nothing and chorus 'I can't find it' each time I ask for rent? You...

ÀBẸ̀KẸ́: If you want to be honest, you will know that this is the first time we have not paid your rent at the proper time. And there is a cause for that.

LANDLORD: And what can that cause be? You think the landlord is dead and has willed this part of his estate to you?

ÀBẸ̀KẸ́: We have never thought of such inheritance. Our rent this month is late because my husband has been fired from his job. *(The landlord looks at Dèyí, puts his pipe in his mouth, smiles demurely, then coughs the big man's cough).*

LANDLORD: My heart breaks to hear that, but that is no excuse for an unpaid rent. My thirteenth building is under construction at Aperin and I need money to pay the workers. Do you think 'my-husband-has-just-been-fired-from-his-job' *(Imitating Abeke's feminine voice)* is legal tender for bricklayers covered with mud and grime? *(Àbẹ̀kẹ́ discovers Toyin eavesdropping behind the curtain. The anxiety registers on her face).*

ÀBẸ̀KẸ́: It is alright now, *Oga* Landlord. You go and we will find your money by all means.

LANDLORD: I live on money, not on promises. *(Laughs deliriously)*. When will the thing rustle in my pocket?
ÀBÈKẸ́: Come next week.
LANDLORD: And if I do and it is not ready, I will throw out all these wretched things you call your property one by one. I mean it! *(Bites his silver-plated watch-strap)*. Ògún gbọ́!*

Lights fade out

---

*Ogun (god of iron) is my witness!

III

Late morning. Àbèké is struggling with her sewing machine as usual. Beside her is a rusty transistor radio, its sound faint from weak batteries. The 'Ìyálèta Programme' is on, and as always, there is little talk but much music. Behind a burst of whirring guitar, the following song can be heard:

>Olówó lòwò, olówó laye mo.
>Olówó mà ni baba.
>Bo bá lówó, o lè mú afẹ̌fẹ̌ dání.
>Bo bá ní sekendí, o lè dá òjò mú o.
>Olówó ḿbò lonà o.
>Enitó bá pa àpagbé. (2ce)

>The rich man is the one the world knows.
>The rich man is boss.
>With money you can trap the wind.
>With money you can stop the rain.
>The rich man is coming.
>He kills with impunity.

Solá and Tóyin are seated on the couch, the latter trying desperately to explain the logic of English Grammar to the former.

	Big, bigger, biggest.
TÒYÍN:	*(Ṣọlá repeats after her)*. Now compare 'good'
ṢỌLÁ:	Good, gooder, goodest.
TÒYÍN:	*(Laughs mockingly)*. How many times shall I tell you that it is 'good, better, best'?
	(Visibly surprised). But why not 'good, gooder, goodest?'
ṢỌLÁ:	I don't know but our teacher says it must be *'good, better, best'*. He said that is how the white man wants us to speak his language. *(The children's grammatical drill is interrupted by the entry of Ìyá Àgbà, an imposing woman, a combination of aplomb and arrogance.)*
TOYIN AND ṢỌLÁ:	Ẹ kaarọ, Ìyá Àgbà.
ÌYÁ ÀGBÀ:	Ẹ kaarọ, ọmọ mi.

        Àkanní, Àdunní, Ajífowówẹ
        Èyin ni mo jí rí loni o.
        (Àkanní, Àdunní who take a daily shower of money,
        You are the first persons I'm seeing upon waking up this morning)
        Àbẹ̀kẹ́ kneels down and greets Ìyá Àgbà. Ìyá Àgbà answers half-heartedly and makes towards the couch which has now been vacated by the kids who disappear through the left door. As she sits, the couch rattles under her.

ÌYÁ ÀGBÀ: Un...un... it is a long time since I came here last. Even your seat complains about my presence.

ÀBĘKĘ́: Yes, Mama I think it is about three weeks now since you came here. On your way to Baba Àrẹ̀mú's house warming ceremony.

ÌYÁ ÀGBÀ: Hun un un *(Rather pensively)*. Where is your husband? How is his work going?

ÀBĘ́KĘ́: He no longer has any.

ÌYÁ ÀGBÀ: *(Unmoved)*. Hen, en en... What happened to his job?

ÀBĘ́KĘ́: He was retre... *(Trying to find the correct pronunciation)*. The Oyinbo and his representative here have told him to stay at home.

ÌYÁ ÀGBÀ: *(Coldly)*. Hun un un. I heard it. They say Dèyí has joined the group of the jobless who play *ayò* (game) before the morning pap and stay on till they cannot see the seeds in the holes. They say your husband is now a member of that gang called Ọmọ ajírinhú, oníbàtàa kúrhbä* (Street wanderer with shoes worn at the heels) He e e e! *(Claps her hands mischievously)*. My son-in-law a jobless husband, the kind who exchanges his *ṣọ́rọ́* (trousers) for his wife's *yẹ̀ẹ̀rì* (skirt) The...

ÀBĘ́KĘ́: Alright Mama, is there anything in particular you want to tell me this morning?

ÌYÁ ÀGBÀ: *(Sits up, literally bracing up for a confrontation)*. What I want to tell you? I thought I told you a lot before, and if you didn't have cotton wool in your ears, you would have heard my words.

ÀBĘ́KĘ́: Mama I...

ÌYÁ ÀGBÀ: Keep quiet and let me talk. When you said you wanted to marry this man, did I not tell you you were getting married to another woman? A lazy man with hair on his palms! You said he worked for a company, an *oyinbo* company.

ÀBÈKẸ́: But I...

ÌYÁ ÀGBÀ: A thousand leaves in your mouth if you don't let me speak my mind! *(Perches on the edge of the couch).* I told you that I-am-working-for-a-company, I-am-working-for-a-company does not allow us to tell the manager *(Pronounced 'Mónijà')* from the ordinary floor sweeper.

ÀBÈKẸ́: Dèyí was not a sweeper. He was a machine operator.

ÌYÁ ÀGBÀ: *Mọsin operator?* Did he go to school to learn it? Where is his *sabukeet. (Certificate)*?

ÀBÈKẸ́: He learned it on the job.

ÌYÁ ÀGBÀ: You can go on trying to cover the smoke of your wretchedness. But everyone now knows that your husband is a jobless person and two kobo cannot jingle in his pocket.

ÀBÈKẸ́: But Mama, in spite of this we still manage. Immediately they heard about retren... *(Unsuccessfully again)...* the thing that happened to Dèyí, his friends put a few naira together and gave it to us. This should give us one good meal a day for about two weeks more.

ÌYÁ ÀGBÀ: Will it also be enough for all the things Dèyí should be doing? For several months now, Dèyí has not given me a kobo. Next month is the 40th day of the 50th anniversáry of Mama Sèkungbólá's father's funeral and we have selected the *aṣọ ẹbí (Communal dress)* for this. My friend, Mama Sali, got the money for the *aṣọ ẹbí* from her daughter, Mama Anikẹ got hers from her son-in-law who is a big government contractor. But where is the son-in-law to do that kind of thing for me?

ÀBẸ̀KẸ́: But that is not only what sons-in-law are for, Mama.

ÌYÁ ÀGBÀ: What else are they for? Just look at where you call a home. *(Surveys the room).* How can I bring my friends to come and see my daughter in this kind of place?

ÀBẸ̀KẸ́: People make places, Mama. You have Toyin, Ṣọlá, Dèyí, and me.

ÌYÁ ÀGBÀ: I would have preferred to have a different son-in-law. And you had all the chances in this world to give me one. You were beautiful and mannerful, and many men were after you. Many men including Alhaji Robo, a government contractor who now rolls in money. He would have made you an Alhaja, selling lace, damask (*Pronounced 'Damaas'*) and *Jábúrẹ́dì* at Gbági. What about Jeremiah, the one who sells *oyìnbó* fine, fine medicine, who owns six houses along Jàkùté Road? You rejected them and chose Dèyí. Like a stubborn leech, you stuck to Dèyí's leg. You

17

	saw a boat that was sure to sink and you decided to thrust your fate upon it.
ÀBÈKÉ:	Mama, you know that Dèyí doesn't deserve this from you. When things were right and he had a job, he performed the duties of a good son-in-law. He...
ÌYÁ ÀGBÀ:	Yes, he bought the car which I now ride, didn't he? He gave me fifty thousand naira to help my trade, didn't he?
ÀBÈKÉ:	That is not all there is to life, Mama. Mama I know we live in a society which measures people's worth by the length of their cars and the cost of their apparels. Dèyí may not have big cars and costly clothes, he has us.

At this point Ṣọlá peeps through the curtain, then walks unsurely towards his mother.

ṢỌLÁ:	I am hungry Mama.
ÀBÈKÉ:	Alright, go and play. When I finish my talk with Màmá Àgbà I will cook and then you can eat. Pèlé, Akanni, go and play. (*Exit Ṣọlá*).
ÌYÁ ÀGBÀ:	Yes now I see what Dèyí has: hungry children and a wife who worships a thirty-year old sewing machine. *(Pause)*. Before I go I have something to tell you.
ÀBÈKÉ:	What is it Mama?
ÌYÁ ÀGBÀ:	Dèyí's course has not profitted you: why not change your route. You are still young and beautiful and many men will like to marry you.

ÀBÈKÉ: And my two children, and the one I carry in my womb? What shall I tell them? That I change husbands because Dèyí is too poor to be their father? No, Mama. I don't know what these children could become tomorrow. I have seen bright stars emerge from a dark sky; small forests have bred elephants.

ÌYÁ ÀGBÀ: Let me go before the elephant in your small forest tramples me. But remember, mother of the coming elephant, hunger and the stomach are not friends. Find something to do about yourself.

Ìyá Àgbà rises, adjusts her 'gèlè', (head gear) thrusts on her ìborùn (shawl draped across the shoulder) and bursts out through the uncurtained entrance. Fade out.

IV

A night club with a small-sized music band playing on the platform. The club is not in full session yet, so some of the seats are empty. At one corner of the hall are seated Dèyí with two friends talking in a low tone. The impressive number of empty bottles on their table shows they must have been drinking for some time.

The leader of the music band beckons a provocatively dressed, rather chesty bar-maid waiting in one corner of the room. She struts in, collects empty bottles and glasses from members of the music band and turns back, wiggling her fulsome behind.

The band leader strums his guitar to nudge his colleagues into action. The music begins and the band leader raises the first song.

Lead: *Olówó ló layé ọ̀rẹ́ mi o* The rich man owns the world
    Owó la fí ńjayé Money is the sauce of life
Chorus: *A o ṣe owo o(2ce)* Money, oh money!
    Owó lè ṣoun gbogbo Money can do everything
Lead: *Owó lará ọrẹ mi o* Money is the best relation
    Òṣì ní jẹ́ taní mọ̀ ọ́ rí Poverty has no friends
Chorus: *A o ṣe owo o (2ce)* Money, oh money!
    Owó le ṣoun gbogbo Money can do everything
Lead: *Owó ní ńpani, owó ní ńla ni* Money kills, money saves

> Owó le sènià d'Ọlọ́run   Money can turn a man
> into God
> Lead: À o ṣe owó o (2ce)   Money, oh money!

At this point, a shortish barrel-bellied man in complete lace suit (ṣọ́rọ́, bùbá, agbádá) enters with a retinue of flatterers. He is literally sandwiched between two plump women, equally gaudilly dressed. The followers variously shout 'Bàbá o!'* 'Àjẹpẹ́ ayé o!'**, etc. As the man enters, the band changes its tune and the leader bursts into a throaty praise song:

> Ẹ bá mi pe baba ńílé   Join me in praising the
> lord of the house
> Baba lóko, baba ní ìbábá   Lord of the farm
> Baba ni bábá   Lord of every nook
> Baba ni ikọ̀kọ̀   Lord of every nook and
> cranny
>
> Òyìnbó iwin inú owó   Wizard of money
> Oyinbo igi tó ńsowó   Wizard tree of money

The man thrusts his right hand into his voluminous agbada pocket and brings out a fat wad of naira, complete with the bank seal. He holds it in the air with both hands to show the appreciative crowd that it is really mint. A roar of 'Baba o!' rents the air. Then the man proceeds towards the platform, tears off the paper band around the wad and begins to 'spray' the band leader. He

---

* Big Daddy!
** Long enjoyment of life!

pastes a couple of notes on his forehead and the sweat there serves as adhesive to keep the notes in place. He slots a few into the space between his head and his ears, rolls up a few and inserts them in his nostrils, stuffs some into his mouth, and then goes on to 'spray' the other band members. Then he digs his hand into his pocket and produces another wad. First he sprays individual foreheads, then throws the rest of the notes in the air. The people jump upon one another to catch them. When the stampede has subsided, the man shouts 'Ótó ó!'(Enough) and there is magic silence. He wipes his fleshy face, and bursts into a song:

Bámú bámú layó (2ce)	We are fully contented (2ce)
Àwa ò mò pé'bi n pọmọ	What business is ours if
enìkan àn kan	others are starving?
Bámú bámú layó	We are fully contented

The band picks up the tune and the crowd hilariously choruses the song several times. The dancing continues in a subdued way as Dèyí's corner now gains focus.

GÒKÈ: Why didn't you rise to pick up your own share, Dèyí?

AKIN: Yes, I saw he was here while the *àríyá (merriment)* was on.

GÒKÈ: As though he was glued to his chair *(laughs softly)*

AKIN: I thought you lost your job, not your legs, as our people say, '*Kójú máa ríbi, ẹsẹ́ loògùn ẹ*'.*

---

* If the eyes are not to see evil, the legs must be alert.

GÒKÈ: You're wrong, Akin, *gbogbo ara lòògùn e.* **
They both laugh but Dèjí maintains a straight face and seems to be totally consumed by his thinking.
DÈYÍ: *(Breaking his silence)* Who's that man?
GÒKÈ: Who?
DÈYÍ: Who else could it be but the one who just performed a public *sàárà*? (public largesse)
AKIN: Oh, you mean you don't know him? That's Chief Kagbade - Jones, the government contractor.
GÒKÈ: He's also the special manufacturer's representative for Wentbury Enterprises with headquarters in London, Paris, New York, and Yokohama.
DÈYÍ: Where did he get all that money? Or were those play bills that he was spraying?
AKIN: Well, I understand he's just won another contract from the government. This time a really fat one; and so he is celebrating the award.
GÒKÈ: Many of the people you are looking at *(points in the direction of the dancers)* knew he would be here today. And so they came to take part in the *sàárà*.
AKIN: Now tell us, why didn't you struggle for your own share? Are you sworn to everlasting poverty?
DÈYÍ: I do not want the tree to fall so that I may pluck its fruit without climbing. I do not want my neighbour's wall to fall on his goat so that I may have meat for my evening meal.
GÒKÈ: Hun un! You are quite a poet.

** .... the whole body must be alert.

AKIN: A perfect wordsmith! If words were money you would surely be a millionaire.

GÒKÈ: Unfortunately, the word market is glutted and so the orator returns home with hunger in his stomach and head heavy with his wares.

AKIN: That *(Pointing to the rich man)* is the poet of our time. The rustle of crisp notes is rhyme in the ears.

GÒKÈ: You see, you think too much, Dèyí, so that you let thinking consume you in addition to hunger. Mind you, it is not that we too don't think. But the point is, we think with the times while you think against the times.

AKIN: Perfectly right. The world grabs what is, you think of what should be. And so your life is ruled by the quest for what never was but should have been. This is why, unlike us, you can't suffer and smile.

DÈYÍ: Frankly, most times I believe I do not belong here.

GÒKÈ: *(Smiling mildly)* Where then do you belong? Are you sure it is better over there?

AKIN: That is the question. Nobody who went there has ever come back to tell us his experience.

GÒKÈ: My grandfather used to say that the battle we know is better than the one we do not know.

AKIN: Yes, the battle is here. And when we run out of ammunition, we ask for the bottle. Hee! Sisi *(calls bar-maid)*. More beer!

As they resume their drinking, the club comes alive again with a whir of guitar and drums and the dancing continues. (Fade out).

V

Dèyí's sitting room. Dèyí sits on the couch as usual. He is in a deeply pensive mood. Àbèké sits beside him, trying to console him.

ÀBÈKÉ: You look very sad, Dèyí. Please try to cheer up.

DÈYÍ: I will try.

ÀBÈKÉ: But you have said that many times without really trying.

DÈYÍ: I went to the labour office yesterday and the workers there treated us like shit: a thing that comes out of you but which you don't want to see.

ÀBÈKÉ: But that was not the first time they have treated you badly. Everybody says they do their work by pulling down the spirit of job seekers.

DÈYÍ: I never knew this could happen to me. A clerk slightly older than Tóyìn calling us beggars who insist on choosing.

ÀBÈKÉ: Why, anything to choose from?

DÈYÍ: Yes, indeed! Menial jobs whose only requirement is that you crawl on your stomach like a snake. Two times now they have offered me jobs as a houseboy- imagine house**boy** *(Stresses boy)*- to an expatriate.

ÀBẸ̀KẸ́: Houseboy?
DÈYÍ: They say because I speak good English.
ÀBẸ̀KẸ́: Don't you tell them you are a machine operator?
DÈYÍ: Yes, I did. But I was told there is no machine to operate unless I set up my own factory.
DÈYÍ: Why is the world as it is? Yesterday's paupers turn millionaires overnight and people hail them in the streets. They hold weekly parties and throw out money like discarded paper.
ÀBẸ̀KẸ́: Those are sacrifices for their crime.
Boys born only yesterday; with little or no education.
ÀBẸ̀KẸ́: But a lot of important connections. It does not depend upon who you are but who you know.
DÈYÍ: That is the saying of our time.

A local radio station's signature tune is heard and the time is announced.

ÀBẸ̀KẸ́: Oh, it is two o'clock. I must go to the market now. This is the time you can get vegetables fresh and cheap.

She dashes out. Dèyí can't even raise up his head to see her depart. At this point the news has started and one of the items goes:

ÀBẸ̀KẸ́: 'The Governor of Apélókó State performed the laying of the foundation of a seventy-five million naira project at Ereki today. It is a joint venture between an overseas company called Richester and a handful of local, enterprising entrepreneurs. The Governor praised the project and called it another brave step towards wiping out unemployment and raising the living standard of every Apelokoan. He described this day as one everyone should be proud of. The election...'

Dèyi switches off the radio and goes off-stage. Moments later, - he reappears, wearing a pair of big rusty boots and a bowler hat. He scribbles something on a piece of paper and puts it on the couch, placing his pen on it to prevent it from getting blown away. He removes his wristwatch and places it besides the paper. Then he goes slowly out through the uncurtained entrance. For a good many seconds, a room empty of people stares at the audience. Then fade out.

VI

Àbèké comes in through the curtained door, talking animatedly as she enters.

ÀBÈKÉ: Dèyí... Dèyí... we are lucky today. I got good vegetables and fish. My friend who sells *Òkú Èkó* (*Frozen fish popularly called Lagos corpse*) gave me some at *ó sè' wọ* (*concessional*) price. *Noticing the lack of response from the inner room, she goes off-stage and races back shouting 'Dèyí... Dèyí'. The piece of paper and wrist-watch on the couch catch her attention and she dashes across, grabs the note, reads it, her hand shaking feverishly, and collapses in the chair, sobbing violently. Toyin and Ṣọlá, coming home from evening classes, meet their mother in this state and rush to her, shouting 'Mama... Mama'. The only coherent statement from Àbèké is 'He's gone, he's gone' which she repeats several times. Tóyìn bursts into tears in sympathy with her mother. Ṣọlá holds her mother's hand but keeps a dry face. The radio announces the hour and starts on the news on the hour. Towards the end the announcer says:*

'And now the last item of the news. The body of a light-skinned man has just been found hanging from an *isin* tree at Mile Twenty near the Oribo Bridge. The man is described as middle-aged and has a fairly large scar on his left arm. The identification found on him shows him as a former worker of Pantibury Overseas Limited. The police are still investigating the circumstances surrounding his death. And now before I go...
Ask not what your country can do for you...

Àbèké's sobbing escalates into profuse weeping. She holds Tóyìn and Sọlá in each hand and presses them close to her breast. Sọlá's face is dry, firm, and far...
A very slow fade out.

THE WEDDING CAR

CHARACTERS

Lazarus
Jèmíná
Chief Nínálowó-Chamberlain
Alàgbà Fágbó Ògúnpàdé
His Wife, Ngozi Ogúnpàdé
Professor Harold Jim-East
Mrs Flora Jim-East
Bride
1st Foil Bride
2nd Foil Bride
Host Woman
Guest Woman
1st Man from groom's party
2nd Man from groom's party
Old Man
Dérèmí the groom
Túnjí his Bestman
Taylor (a.k.a. Toronto Cuts)
Lásún
Two Customs Officers
Drummers, singers, dancers

I

(A loud, enthusiastic song rises off-stage, gradually filling up the theatre):

Call:	Kí lè ńsee tì e fi pò báàyí	What celebration brings
Response:	Ìyàwó là ńgbé ooo	you out in such large
Call:	Ìlèkè so, Ìlèkè so wòwò	numbers
Response:	Ìyàwó là ńgbé ooo	We are out for a wedding.
		Cascade of beads,
		Cascade of beads,
		We are out for a wedding.

(The lights reveal a large sitting room furnished in a grotesquely opulent way. The walls are decorated with family photographs. In a corner hangs a large picture of Jesus Christ on the Cross. There is a general flurry of activities: people moving in and out, shifting tables and chairs, trying to get the room ready for a great gathering. Lazarus and Jemina, houseboy and housegirl respectively, are cleaning up the heavily upholstered chairs).

LAZARUS: *(Showing signs of fatigue, tries to stand erect, one of his hands holding his lower back. He grimaces painfully and yawns loudly. As he speaks the background music subsides).* O o o o h! Good Lord!

JÈMÍNÁ: *(Straightening up and shooting a glance at Lazarus)* Lazarus, what's the matter? Are you alright?

LAZARUS: Y e e e s. *(But feeling the pain again.)* No o. It's this back of mine. Just as if somebody has stuck a thousand needles in it.

JÈMÍNÁ: It's no needles, Lazarus. It is overwork. Remember we have not had a minute's rest for the past three days.

LAZARUS: I know. This house servant work is slave work. Next time I come to this world, I will not do any silly servant work. No, I have done all my slave work in this life. I too want to be a master *(Posing)* with a well-nourished big belly sitting on my belt, a beautiful house *(Surveys the room)* in a quiet corner of the town, complete with a gate and a gateman, a large board saying: 'BEWARE OF THE DOG', and a dozen servants taking messages to uncountable concubines. Listen to me, God, I too want to know what it is like at the owner's corner of a Mercedes-Benz.

JÈMÍNÁ: Looks like you are well already! Dreams are a good cure for backache. Now that you have come down from your Mercedes, you have landed on the hard floor of Chief Nínálowó-Chamberlain's sitting room where you are a houseboy! *(They both laugh, momentarily returning to their cleaning).*

LAZARUS: Honestly, this servant work is the worst in the world.

JÈMÍNÁ: I know. You are the last to sleep.

LAZARUS: And the first to wake up.

JÈMÍNÁ: You cook business breakfast.

LAZARUS: And contract luncheons.

JÈMÍNÁ: You prepare christening feasts.

LAZARUS: And birthday feasts.

JÈMÍNÁ: House-warming parties.

LAZARUS: And funeral feasts.

JÈMÍNÁ: And if, by chance, Master doesn't have any ceremony on a weekend, he lends you out to his friends who do.

LAZARUS: You cook the food.

JÈMÍNÁ: But you eat the left-over.

(A voice is heard from off-stage. The two resume their cleaning, mistaking the approaching voice for Chief Ninálowó-Chamberlain's).

JÈMÍNÁ: I thought he was coming.

LAZARUS: Me too.

JÈMÍNÁ: For all this suffering just imagine what you get at the end of the month!

LAZARUS: I earn two thousand naira a month, the same amount I started with here five years ago.

JÈMÍNÁ: That buys only two bottles of whisky. Remember how many bottles we have stocked up for this wedding!

LAZARUS: That money merely passes through your hands into other hands. By the time you send money to your mother, grandmother, brothers, sisters, and several others, you are left with virtually nothing. Just see, this shoe is seven years old; it has seen the inside of every shoemaker's shop in this town. Yet its heels are so worn that when I walk, it is like the desperate struggle of an *asòpá* (one with swollen testicles) *(demonstrates)*.

JÈMÍNÁ: The price of everything has gone up: *gaàrí* is untouchable, only rich people and senators now eat rice. Yet whenever you ask for more pay, what you get is threat, threat, threat. *(posing)* More pay? What work do you do that you now want a thousand naira a month? If you are not careful I will just send you away. You know there are thousands out there wishing to work for half your salary.

LAZARUS: I am tired of this job, but I don't know where else to go. *(Pause)* When I grow up and I have my own children, I will do everything to educate them-in college, in university, even if I will have to sell my clothes to do it. No, my children will not carry the urine and shit of other people and be kicked in the arse like a donkey. When they shout 'houseboy!', my son will not answer 'Yes Sir!'.

(Both resume their cleaning, their hands moving to the rhythm of the song:)

      Ẹrú mà ní baba ò   The slave has a father
      Ẹrú mà ní baba   The slave has a father
      Ọ̀nà ló jìnà o   Only that he is so far away
      Ẹrú mà ní baba   The slave has a father

(Fade-out)

II

(A wedding song rises off-stage and continues for some time. The lights reveal Chief Nínálowó-Chamberlain's sitting room. Seated here are Chamberlain himself, Prof. Harold Jim-East and his wife, Alàgbà Fágbó Ògúnpàdé and his wife Ngozi and two or three other friends of the Chamberlain family. Chamberlain is clad in ṣọ́rọ́, bùbá, and agbádá, made of expensive lace or 'jankad' material, his neck bedecked with beads of assorted shapes and colours. Prof. Jim-East is in an out-dated English suit, his wife wears a frock complete with hat and gloves. Alàgbà Ògúnpàdé and his wife are in modest but attractive ankara. The others flourish so self-consciously in expensive aṣọ-ẹbí. There is an audible bustle off-stage: pounding, grinding, singing, chattering, etc. Mrs Chamberlain struts in with matronly gait, whispers something in her husband's ear and quickly disappears).

CHIEF CHAMBERLAIN: I have just been told that the wedding car is ready and is parked outside.

(Everyone rushes to the window. There are approbative nods and grunts, and praise names of the Mercedes: Òbòkún Bàbá!, Mẹ̀ẹ̀sí Ọlóyẹ́, Oníbèbè Pọnbé Kọ́rọ́bọ́tọ́ bí ọká, etc. Then they return to their seats).

CHIEF CHAMBERLAIN: There it is. I have always nursed the hope that my daughter will answer the wedding bell in the most expensive car in the country. You can see the colour is white; I like white; it is the colour of angels.

ALÀGBÀ ÒGÚNPÀDÉ: How the times have changed! Remember, Aina, we went to the marriage registry by foot—some five miles or so from where we lived as school teachers.

PROF. JIM-EAST: Indeed that was a long time ago. Things are different now. I attended a wedding in Lagos last week where people had so much champagne that they emptied dozens of bottles into a large bowl and washed their hands in it.

ALÀGBÀ ÒGÚNPÀDÉ: But I understand champagne is banned.

CHIEF CHAMBERLAIN: Yes, to those who don't know their way around. You see, nobody bans anything in this country unless he has already secured a channel for his personal supply. *(Enter two servants, one carrying assorted wines and whiskies on a large tray, the other following with a tray of glasses. They serve and exit. Then a young woman brings in a bowl of fried meat which she places on a low table in the centre of the room. The party help themselves to it)*

MADAM NGOZI ÒGÚNPÀDÉ: So many times I have asked myself, 'Why are weddings so expensive these days?' Many families have gone into crippling debt to finance weddings. The whole drama lasts less than two hours but the young couple may spend the first ten years of their life together trying to clear the debt. It's sheer madness, and I think something ought to be done about it. Our people should be taught the difference between wedding and marriage.

PROF. JIM-EAST: It is the fashion of our times; besides, I think such weddings add colour and variety to life. Life would be poorer without them.

ALÀGBÀ ÒGÚNPÀDÉ: Life is already poorer because of them. People embezzle public funds to finance weddings. Not long ago, a young man commited armed robbery to raise money for his wedding.

CHIEF CHAMBERLAIN: Really? Incredible!

MADAM ÒGÚNPÀDÉ: It may sound incredible, but it was in the newspapers.

CHIEF CHAMBERLAIN: Then what happened to him?

ALÀGBÀ ÒGÚNPÀDÉ: He was sentenced to death.

MADAM ÒGÚNPÀDÉ: And a few weeks later his bride-to-be ran off with the man who should have been the bestman at the wedding.

PROF. JIM-EAST: No, no. All these minor incidents apart, I think wedding parties, no matter how expensive, are really worth it.

MRS JIM-EAST: Yes, you see, it is like birth and death, you only experience it once.

MADAM ÒGÚNPÀDÉ: Of course, Flora, you know that's untrue. These days people get married as many times as please their whims..

PROF. JIM-EAST: As professor and social philosopher, I know what weddings do to the social fabric. Look at Britain. She forgot all those headaches ... all those unrests ... the demonstrations, the arsons, lootings, etc, and gave her Prince a worthy wedding. For once the country felt like a nation Oh! those jubilant crowds, those banners, those anthems ... oh Rule Britannia!

ALÀGBÀ ÒGÚNPÀDÉ: Come back home, professor *(General laughter)*. I'm sure you know there are people who smashed their television sets when the pictures of the royal wedding came up on the screen. With due respect, Professor, weddings have not been known to eradicate poverty and hunger and disease. In fact, such ostentatious weddings increase the anger of the poor, the real victims of the extravagance.

(The discussion is interrupted by a group of drummers who enter from stage left. The 'gangan' man drums out the following song)

Olówó lọ́rẹ́ ti wa	We are only friends of the rich
Olówó lọ́rẹ́ ti wa	We are only friends of the rich
Ẹní bá tòsì	Let the poor
Kó dákú forí sọlẹ̀	Dash their heads on the ground
Olówó lọ́rẹ́ ti wa	We are only friends of the rich

The crowd constitutes a lively chorus. Chief Chamberlain and others merely nod their heads, but about half a dozen women come on stage, dancing vigorously. Chamberlain rises and pastes several currency notes on the foreheads of the dancing women. The drummers change their tune, now concentrating on Chamberlain's 'Oríkì':

Níná lowó ọmọ ọlọ́lá	Ninalowo, man of wealth,
Ọmọ ọlọ́lá	Man of riches
Ọmọ afowó-pani-gbéni-sin	One who kills and oppresses with money.
Ọmọ Ákégun Àtàngà	
Tó pẹni méje láàrọ̀	Son of Akégun Àtàngà
Tó bẹ́rí ogbọ̀n nírọ̀lẹ́	Who killed seven people at dawn,
Ó délé tán	Beheading thirty at dusk.
Ó délé tán	Getting home,
Ó ní áà, Ogun ò rí nkan jẹ	He said the massacre was not enough
Igba ẹrú ló sin bàbá ẹ̀	Hundreds of slaves served your father
Igba iwọfà ló nkoko àna rẹ.	Hundreds of serfs till your in-law's land

(Chamberlain's head swells. He rises enthusiastically from his seat, digs his hand into his voluminous pocket, brings out a wad of notes which he pastes on the lead drummer's forehead. The music tempo rises, Chamberlain digs both hands into his pocket, brings out several wads and 'sprays' the notes indiscriminately on the heads of

all the drummers. There is a loud shout of approbation. Then he starts to dance, the women cheering him and spreading their head-ties on the ground for him to walk upon. Moments later the crowd dance off-stage, followed by the drummers. Then Chamberlain returns to his former seat).

PROF. JIM-EAST: Ah, Chief, that was fantastic!

MRS. JIM-EAST: Yes, indeed! You danced as if that's what you do for a living.

CHIEF CHAMBERLAIN: *(Breathing hard)* Thank you. No, I do other things for a living! E e e, yes, as we were saying, there are different reasons why people float expensive parties. You people talk about social fabric and all that. I am not a book man; I know little about social fabric. But as a businessman and politician, I know nobody holds expensive parties for nothing. Yes, nobody, because as our people say, for every finger you point, there are three others looking in your direction. When a businessman floats a party, he invites other businessmen who not only bring rich gifts, but also bring friends and other businessmen with extensive connections. So parties and other ceremonies provide a forum for contact, *(Pause)* and contract. For us businessmen, parties are a sacrifice, and an investment; we count our profits, when the empty bottles are back in the cartons.

ALÀGBÀ ÒGÚNPÀDÉ: So this is why ......

CHIEF CHAMBERLAIN: Now, before you get me wrong, let me add that there are other reasons for making my daughter's wedding so elaborate. You all know Tokunbo is my eldest daughter, and one that I am very fond of. No amount is too great to spend on her wedding. Besides, I am sure you know that I have won a fifty-million naira contract to kill all the rats in the new capital city. This party is partly a celebration of that. And as those drummers said, I come from a family of great men and great doers. My great, great-grandfather was a wealthy warrior who feasted the whole town several times in a year. So, you see we have a great tradition which I must keep alive.

PROF. JIM-EAST: Talking about guests and connections, how many important people are coming to the wedding?

CHIEF CHAMBERLAIN: Uncountable!

MADAM ÒGÚNPÀDÉ: The President?

CHIEF CHAMBERLAIN: No, he's away in Switzerland, but he sent his own gift.

ALÀGBÀ ÒGÚNPÀDÉ: His Vice?

CHIEF CHAMBERLAIN: Yes surely. You know he's married to the daughter of Chief *Agbàlówómeri*, one of the principal shareholders in our company.

MRS JIM-EAST: The Vice-Chancellor?
CHIEF CHAMBERLAIN: Will surely come. He has even made the university hall available for the reception. You still remember that I was one of those who helped him to get the post.
MADAM ÒGÚNPÀDÉ: The Governor?
CHIEF CHAMBERLAIN: Actually three governors are coming. I got their acceptances two weeks ago.
PROF. JIM-EAST: Senators?
CHIEF CHAMBERLAIN: Yes, many of them, and representatives and assemblymen.
MADAM ÒGÚNPÀDÉ: The Army Chief?
CHIEF CHAMBERLAIN: He declined the invitation, saying that he will feel strange in the company of *agbada* men who now run the show. He would rather keep to the barracks.
MRS JIM-EAST: Officiating clergy?
CHIEF CHAMBERLAIN: The Archbishop cannot conduct the service; he's still recovering from the fatigue of the recent royal wedding. But he has directed the Bishop to select the best clergy to handle the job. *(Pause)* Lazarus!
LAZARUS *(Hurrying on stage)* Yesah!
CHIEF CHAMBERLAIN: Tell all the women to hurry up their cooking. The engagement party will soon be here. It's 10 o'clock by my time, *abi*?
(Searches the faces of those around to confirm the accuracy of his time. They nod in agreement)

(To Lazarus) Is Mama Tokunbo there?
LAZARUS: Yesah! She has been working very hard, cooking, frying....
CHIEF CHAMBERLAIN: O. K. Give her the message.
LAZARUS: Yesah!
CHIEF CHAMBERLAIN: *(With a self-congratulatory air)* Talking about connections, do you know I got all the rice for this party free?
PROF. JIM-EAST: Really?
CHIEF CHAMBERLAIN: Yes!
MRS JIM-EAST: But how?
CHIEF CHAMBERLAIN: The how is as plain as the palm of your hand: if you know the right people, nothing is impossible in this country. About four weeks ago, I came back from work to find fifty bags of rice stacked up near my garage. Real long-grain American rice, not the *pẽtẽpẽtẽ* thing they call rice in this country. On reading the letter which accompanied it, I discovered the rice came from an old friend I had helped when he was a Grade II teacher running for senate. Many people had thought he had no chance at all against a young lecturer with a bagful of degrees who taught in one of the universities. But eh e eh...., we plugged the right holes and our man won and our university bookman *(Prof. Jim-East explodes a raucous laughter)* lost his

deposit. For a long time I didn't hear from my teacher-friend, until those bags came.

ALÀGBÀ ÒGÚNPÀDÉ: It is the sign of the times. I understand the easiest way to measure a politician's status today is to count the bags of rice stacked up in his house.

MADAM ÒGÚNPÀDÉ: But this rice was imported from America to feed the people.

CHIEF CHAMBERLAIN: Am I not the people ... eh ... eh ... eh., one of the people?

ALÀGBÀ ÒGÚNPÀDÉ: No, the poor people.

CHIEF CHAMBERLAIN: Oh that again! I thought you people were too old to be socialists!

MADAM ÒGÚNPÀDÉ: But the truth is that those who need this rice never get it.

CHIEF CHAMBERLAIN: Truth is bitter and when truth is mixed with rice, it is difficult to swallow. *(Pause)* You see, let those poor people you talk about eat what they get. Our country has not reached that stage where everyone can have enough.

ALÀGBÀ ÒGÚNPÀDÉ: Indeed! If we don't have enough food to go round now, we may have enough trouble to go round later. A country in which a few feed while the majority merely watches is in a state of undeclared war.

MRS JIM-EAṢT: By the way, please let us know how much rice is left after the wedding. We ... *A loud song rises outside the theatre)*

Àwà l'ègbéeoníyàwó	We are the bridal party
Ègbẹ olówó /2ce	A prosperous bunch
Àwà kìí jewúro	We do not eat *ewuro* vegetables
Àfẹ̀jà díndín	
Àwà kìí s'akúṣẹẹ	Only fried fish
A figò lọsọ	We are not of the penurious stock Who iron clothes with the bottle.

(Chamberlain calls Lazarus and tells him to tell the women the engagement party has arrived. The party troops in, singing and dancing, the women leading, carrying assorted goods (yams - really big ones - bales of clothes, etc. in big baskets, calabashes and metal trays. They file past the audience, and as they reach the approaches of the theatre, their host troops in from back stage. The men join Chamberlain's group, the women move forward to meet the guests. Both parties are clad in assorted aṣọ-ẹbí some of which are so transparent that the wearers, underwears are obscenely visible. As both parties meet at the approaches of the stage, the singing and dancing intensify for a while, then die down. The women of the engagement party move forward to commence a dialogue with their hosts, while the men chatter and laugh inaudibly at some distance behind them).

HOSTS: Who are you?
GUESTS: We are of Awórelé family.

HOSTS:	Where are you from?
GUESTS:	We are from Òkè Àràsá.
HOSTS:	What are you here for?
GUESTS:	To request your permission to take the beautiful flower in your house.
HOSTS:	Okay. You're free to cut a rose or a hibiscus in the compound. Or do you want the seeds?
GUESTS:	No please. We've come to ask you to kindly allow your daughter to marry our son.
HOSTS:	That is a big request, and an expensive one too. Have you enough money to support your request?
GUESTS:	We have come here fully prepared. *(A hefty, lavishly endowed woman brusquely emerges from the host group wielding a white piece of chalk)*
WOMAN:	Let's see if you really are. This is white chalk, symbol of the magnificence and purity of the Chamberlain family. Every grain of this chalk is money, its dust is gold. *(Drawing a line to mark off the guest party)* Now prove your strength. This line is worth five thousand naira.

A VOICE FROM THE HOST GROUP: No! Seven thousand!

WOMAN:	Yes, you are right. Seven thousand naira. You must pay before crossing this line.

(The guest party lay heads together, and within seconds, a woman counts out the required sum and hands it over saying):

GUEST WOMAN: Here it is. Seven thousand naira. Fresh from the bank. Yours will be one of the first hands to touch its crisp purity. We want our bride and not even one million naira can keep us away *(to her people)* àbí ...?

(The guests break into a jubilant wedding song and advance a few feet before they are stopped again)

HOST WOMAN: *Ó tóóó!* (Halt!) We have come to a sacred spot in Chamberlain's compound. Here is where Papa Churchill Roosevelt Alade Chamberlain, the first agent of Y and B Foreign Holdings in the whole of this region, was buried. This is a spot to honour if you want his great grand daughter to be your wife. *(Stretching out her hand stylishly).* Five thousand naira only.

(Again the guests lay heads together and offer the money. Singing and dancing once more).

HOST WOMAN: *(As the parties reach the door) Ó tóóó!* (Halt!) Here is the door to Chamberlain's house. It is made of gold, the hinges are of purest silver. When it opens, it is only to let in money. This is the door no poor or wretched dare touch.

(Stretching out her hand) Four thousand naira.

(The guests, their anxiety already becoming visible, lay heads together and offer the money. Then the parties enter the room where Chamberlain and several others are seated. The guests, setting down their burdens, stand on one side of the stage,

the host women on the other. Another woman steps out of the host group and takes up command).

HOST WOMAN: *Ẹ káàbọ̀ o. (You are welcome)* By the way, what did you say you have come to do?

GUESTS: To ask you to allow your daughter to marry our son.

HOST WOMAN: *E e e. (Looks back at her own group who burst into loud laughter).* Do you know her?

GUESTS: Y e e e s.

HOST WOMAN: *O dá a (Alright)*. I will go for her.

GUEST: Thank you, please go.

HOST WOMAN: *(laughing derisively)* A a a ah! Look at them. Where do you think you are? You never had a climbing rope, you never went up the palm-tree, yet reaching the bottom of the palm tree, you tilt back your head and open your mouth. Do you think palm-wine falls free like the rain? *Óyá á!* (Quickly) Five thousand naira for taxi fare!

A VOICE FROM THE HOST GROUP: You will certainly need more. Or do they want you to bring their bride in *alùpandùgbẹ̀* (a rickety vehicle)?

HOST WOMAN: Thank you, my friend, I miscalculated. Five thousand five hundred naira, *Óyá á!* (Quickly!)

(The guests lay heads together again and rake up the money, their enthusiasm diminishing. Moments later, the woman returns with a lace-clad young lady in a

51

veil.) Here is your bride at last. *(Noticing scepticism on the guests' faces)* Why ... why? Don't you like her? Look at them. I climbed seven mountains and crossed nine rivers to bring her. Don't you like her?

GUESTS: No, this is not our bride.

HOST WOMAN: How do you know? You haven't even seen her face.

GUEST WOMAN: When a hunter has been long in the forest, he doesn't see a deer and call it an antelope. We know the gait of our bride; the size of the breast that will suckle our children, the size of the buttocks she will sit upon while rocking our baby. These have been the objects of our worship for three years now. This is not our bride. *(Host Woman removes the veil, and there is a loud shout and laughter)*.

HOST WOMAN: Don't blame me, for I do not mean to deceive you. The girl was already dressed up and veiled when I got to the other end. So I just picked her up and brought her along. If that is not your bride then we must start negotiations afresh. Do you want me to go back for your bride?

GUEST: Ye e e s!

HOST WOMAN: Then this time I will go by train. And you know that costs more *(Stretching her hand)*. Six thousand naira.

(The guests, visibly agitated, take a long time putting the money together. Host Woman takes it and returns seconds later with another young lady).
Here she is, your lovely bride.

GUEST WOMAN: We have opened these eyes for long, and we can tell the colour of fresh clay from that of a five-year old cooking pot. The one we have come for is *Adú-mára-dán oníbàdi òréke* Please go for our bride.

(Again the host unveils the impostor. There is resounding laughter)

HOST WOMAN: I think I will have to go again, like the incompetent messenger burdened with repeated errands. And if I am not tired of going, you should not be tired of sending me. But this time, I want my journey to be fast. You have stood for a long time and I know your legs are tired. To bring your bride swiftly, I want to go by plane. *(Stretching out her hand)* Ten thousand naira.

(The simmering tension in the guest party explodes into a feeling of outrage and disbelief. The bride groom, Dérèmí, bursting through the reins of his family, attempts to walk out, thus causing a brief but troubled exchange in the groom's party)

DÉRÈMÍ: Haba! I came here for a bride, not for a debt to last a lifetime. Just imagine how much these people have squeezed out of us! What do they think we are? Businessmen? Contractors or what?

A MAN FROM THE GUEST PARTY: Cool down your anger, Dérẹ̀mí. Weddings are debts nowadays.

DÉRẸ̀MÍ: No, but I know how many girls our family has given away. If we were like these people we would all be millionaires by now.

MAN: *F'arabalẹ̀*: (Cool down) Everything will be alright.

DÉRẸ̀MÍ: I don't have ten thousand. If they can't go for the bride, I will. I know where Tokunbo is.

(*While this confusion goes on in the guest party, the hosts burst into song:*)

Olówó fara mọ́n mi	Let only the rich stay
Fara mọ́n mi o, fara mọn mi	close to me,
Kó 'tòsi gbéra rẹ̀ lọ	Stay close, stay close
Gbé ra rẹ̀ lọ ò kétékété	Let the poor flee my sight
Eó nán mo rín min ijàyé òní o	Flee, flee absolutely.
Ó dulé iyàwó o o.	It is money that rules today's world
	To the bride's place straight we go.

(*The guests rake the sum together in fives and tens. An old man turns his pockets inside out, gesturing his hands in a frantic "nothing-left" manner. Another man turns out his pocket but tenaciously clutches a ten-naira note*).

2ND MAN: (*When asked to contribute the last ten naira*). Must I starve because my brother's daughter is getting married? Look, I have three wives and twelve children. None of us has had a good meal for three days. You know what *gari* says in the market, don't you? I will not sell all my rags to enrich the man with the silk robe. Our in-laws live in an ocean of wealth; why must we strain for tears to increase its water? Nothing, I repeat, nothing can separate me and this little that I am left with. *(Raising his hand to stress the point)* Ògún gbọ́! (Ògún is my witness!).

(The guests finally rake the money together, and hand it over to the Host Woman who returns moments later with another 'bride').

HOST WOMAN: Here we are again, here is your bride. *(The guests move closer for a brief scrutiny. They exchange glances and declare her to be the real bride. The veil is removed. Everyone, except a few in the guest party, breaks into enthusiastic clapping and singing.)*

Ìyàwó, ẹlẹ́sẹ̀ osùn	Oh bride, with legs adorned with
Inú wá dùn un	camwood
Láti rí ojú rẹ	How happy we are
A ti ná wó	To see your face
A ti ná ra	We have spent money
Inú wa dùn un	We have expended energy
Láti rí ojú rẹ	How happy we are
	To see your face.

(The guest party now take their seats, still singing. Another woman from the bride's family steps forward).

HOST WOMAN: Now you have seen your bride, or our daughter rather, for she is not yours until we have seen the things you have brought. Where are the yams to show us that our daughter will not starve in your house? Where are the clothes to prove that she will have enough to wear and enough to support babies on her back?

A WOMAN FROM THE GROOM'S FAMILY: Here they are in abundance. We are a family that produce yams which challenge the mountain; we have hands that nurture all things that life needs to be full and rich. Our family is an ant-hill of splendid deeds.

(The host counts the articles naming each one as she touches it: yam, alligator pepper, kolanut, salt, honey/ sugar, palm-oil... and the Bible).

A VOICE FROM THE HOST GROUP: Correct?!

HOST WOMAN: Ye e e s, I think so. *(Turning to Tokunbo)* Ìbàdíàrań, ọmọajífọláwẹ̀, ọmọajífowósanwó, these are the things brought by the family of your husband-to-be. I will now call on you to pick out whatever article you consider most valuable of this lot.

(Tokunbo moves forward and mechanically picks out the Bible. Everyone claps and Chief Chamberlain raises a song, others join in:

Àtèmi àtiléè mi	I and my household,
Ọba Olúwa làwa ó ma sin	We shall worship God Almighty day and night
Àtọsán àt'òru	
Ọba Olúwa làwa ó má sin	The God that gave me money
Ọba tó fún mi lówó	
Tó fún mi láṣọ	Who provided my clothing
Ọba Olúwa làwa ó ma sín	We shall worship God Almighty.

HOST WOMAN: *(When the singing and clapping has subsided).* We are glad Tokunbo has shown everyone here the kind of upbringing she had. Of all these, she chose the Bible. You are a good example of our family, an honest, kind-hearted, and *(looking in the direction of Christ's picture on the wall)* a very Christianly family. May God, the Lord of Hosts, Husband of the Widow, Wife of the Bachelor, Food of the Hungry, Wealth of the Poor, whose book you have chosen always be with you and give you money.

(A thunderous response of 'Amen', 'Àṣẹ'. At this stage, the serving of food and drinks has begun: large bowls of iyan, amala, ẹkọ and móínmóín etc. and heavy pots of soup. As the eating commences, Chief Chamberlain rises to speak).

CHIEF CHAMBERLAIN: Today is a happy day for me not only because my first daughter is getting engaged, but also because I have lived to share this happiness with a daughter I love very, very much. Tokunbo has always occupied an important room in my life. She was born when I was studying Accountancy in Newcastle, and her warm company saw us through the terrible winters of England. Since her youth, she has cultivated those virtues of truthfulness, kindness, and compassion that I cherish as her God-fearing father. I have thought about a thousand ways of rewarding her, and finally decided to do her the honour of going to her wedding service in the most expensive car in the country.

(As he speaks he moves towards the window, the people trooping after him. There is a greedy gaze across the window and approbative ejaculations such as Dansaki!', 'Àkíikà!', Funfunleyéisu!', 'Mèsí Oloye!', etc)

Yes, it came by special order from Europe, and tomorrow my daughter will be the first person to sit in its owner's corner.

VOICE FROM THE CROWD: *Bàbá kéẹ*! Son of the Elephant who inherits strength, the big man who does big things!

(At this very moment a hoarse song rises off stage, and an army of beggars enters singing:

Yara su laila   Give us alms
Yara su laila a   In the name of God
Ẹ bùn wá, Ẹ bùn wá   Give us alms.
Nítorí Ọlọ́run   In the name of God
Yara su laila.

(As they come on stage, the crowd spring back in disgust. Each of the beggars grabs a plate of food and begins to eat furiously. Chief Chamberlain calls in two hefty men who hound the beggars off stage, the victims falling over one another in the process. They all return to their seats. An old man in the bride's family rises painfully and moves towards the centre).

OLD MAN   *(Beckoning to Dérẹ̀mí and Tokunbo)* Come here. Kneel down, both of you. *(He prays)*
Your sun which has risen today
May it not set abruptly.

Response: *Àṣẹ*

OLD MAN: The aeroplane never collides
With a tree in the sky
May your life together
Never collide with a rock

Response: *Àṣẹ*

OLD MAN: There are many enemies today
Enemies on the right
Enemies on the left
Enemies in the centre
Enemies that you see
Enemies that you do not see
May their evil hands never reach you

	For, clean does the chicken
	Come out of a forest of thorns.
Response:	*Àṣẹ*
OLD MAN:	Your clouds will become rain
	Whoever says no
	May the rain fall in his stomach
Response:	*Àṣẹ*
OLD MAN:	None can count the seeds
	In the pod of the alligator pepper
	May your children be uncountable
Response:	*Àṣẹ*
OLD MAN:	None can count the sands
	On the seashore
	May your money be uncountable
Response:	*Àṣẹ*
OLD MAN:	May your houses be uncountable
Response:	*Àṣẹ*
OLD MAN:	May your cars be uncountable
Response:	*Àṣẹ*
OLD MAN:	Whoever looks at you with a bad eye
	May that eye vanish from his head
Response:	*Àṣẹ*

CHIEF CHAMBERLAIN: *(After Old Man has resumed his seat)*. Thank you, *Bàbá, kẹ́ẹ gbó, kẹ́ẹ tọ́ọ́*. *(To the people)* Thank you all for your support. Please the party has not ended. Feel free to ask for anything. *Ire á kárí o*. Don't forget, tomorrow morning is the wedding.

(A joyous song bursts out among the groom's party accompanied by vigorous drumming and dancing):

Wọ́n fún wà	We've been given
Wọ́n fún wa	We've been given
Wọ́n fún wa ni Tokun	We've been given Tokun
Wọ́n fún wa ni Tokun	We've been given Tokun
Wọ́n fún wa ni Tokun o	We've been given Tokun
Ká' fí ṣaya.	To be our wife.

Black Out

III

Second day; morning. Wedding day. Wedding bells in the background. Déręmí's room. Sparsely furnished but equipped with a large standing mirror. The walls are decorated with pictures of revolutionary figures - Marx, Lenin, Castro, Che Guevera, Mandela, etc - and those of popular musicians. There is disco music in the background. With Déręmí is Túnjí, his bestman, smoking a cigarette.

TÚNJÍ: My God! that was a real skinning they gave you yesterday. I never knew you would survive it.

DÉRĘMÍ: Withold your surprise. I really haven't survived, and I'm not likely to for the next five years. You know, all those sums extorted from my poor relations, I'll pay back every damned kobo.

TÚNJÍ: I mean ..., it is horrible what intolerable jamborees weddings have become. Just trust our people to overdo everything. People go into debt over funerals, house-warmings, side-turnings, even birthdays. You know what, Déręmí, I'm scared of getting married! *(Both laugh softly)*

DÉRĘMÍ: No, not so bad. Depends upon what family you're dealing with. The problem with me is that I'm caught in the trap of a money-chewing machine of a family who ...

TÚNJÍ: You set that trap for yourself. Remember how many girls were dying to take your hand but you opted for Tokunbo because her father has plenty of money. You see, what you don't know is that when a poor man marries a girl from a wealthy family, the wife's family may take the trousers from the man and give him the skirt of their daughter. *(Again they laugh)*

DÉRẸMÍ: No, none will relieve me of my trousers. No matter how rich my wife is, she can't buy the dynamite between my thighs!

TÚNJÍ: The Major-General himself! I know how many times the domestic superintendent changed your bed in our university days. To this day, we are still surprised how you made your B. A.

DÉRẸMÍ: That was a long time. Now I've changed. Or rather the problems of life have changed me. Talking seriously, do you know I took a five hundred thousand naira loan for this wedding? *(Túnjí expresses surprise)*. Yes half a million. Well, minus the bank manager's ten percent. Now that is all gone!

TÚNJÍ: How ...how managed!

DÉRẸMÍ: How managed? The clothes my dad wore to that engagement, I bought them for him; the ones my mum wore, I also bought.

	Neither had any decent thing to put on their backs. I'm responsible for the entertainment of all the guests from our own side. I have slaughtered three cows already.
TÚNJÍ:	My God! You're in hot soup. How will you pay this back? You are on Level 09.
DÉRÈMÍ:	Actually on Level 08, Step 3.

(The tailor enters, a short, cheery man with an eternal grin! His tape goes round the back of his neck and comes down his chest in two equal rows. He wears a tight fitting dress with multiple pockets, sufficiently intricate to advertise the sophistication of his art.)

TAILOR: *(Heaving his burden on the table).* Here are your suits. Eh, friends, be prepared to wear the best suits in town. The product of busy days and sleepless nights. I tell you, this stuff is very tough; it broke needles endlessly.

(Dérèmí and Túnji try on the dress: the trousers, the flamboyantly embroidered shirts, the waistcoats with gold chains, and tailcoats. Dérèmí opens his wardrobe and produces two bow ties, two bowler hats and two pairs of white gloves. Elegantly spruced up, each looks at the mirror.)

TAILOR: *(Jubilant)* Ó le e jù u! (Fantastic) It's as if you wore this from the womb, as if God was your tailor. No, you look perfect. The bride will surely like this; Uncle Túnjí, the Chief Bridesmaid will run away with you today!

DÉRÈMÍ: Thank you very much, Toronto Cuts. I think this is just perfect. *(After a brief pause)*

TAILOR: I followed the pattern you gave ... plus the pictures I saw in the History books we used in the primary school.

DÉRÈMÍ: *(Absentmindedly)*: Yeah! that's good.

TAILOR: *(Stretching out his hand) Ògá! (Dérèmí pulls one of the drawers and gives the tailor an envelope)*

DÉRÈMÍ: I know. I will give you the balance after the wedding.

TAILOR: Ògá, let your yes be yes and your no be no. Because gàrí dear o, and you big big boss never let us see rice chop.
(Exit)

(Almost instantly, Lásún enters, a tall, composed man carrying a small bag in one hand and a camera slung across his shoulders. He also carries a fanciful pipe which he seldom smokes)

LÁSÚN: *(Taken aback by his friends' costumes)* Eh men! What's this? You look like oversized penguins!

DÉRÈMÍ: *(Ignoring his remarks)* E e h, Lásún. Nice to see you. I never thought you would make it.

TÚNJÍ: Where have you been? You look so fresh! I'm sure there must be about a dozen women cooking òbòkún (choicest fish) for you

DÉRẸMÍ: You can trust the former 'John Thomas' of Kuje Hall, unless he has changed.

LÁSÚN: Which is what he has. You see, growing up poses several challenges which have superceded the frivolities of salad days.

DÉRẸMÍ & TÚNJÍ: *Òyìnbó pọ!* (Copious English)

LÁSÚN: Yes, remember I took a Combined Honours in English and Classics. I know the roots and branches of words. I can trace their etymological and morphological propensities ... *(They all laugh)*.

TÚNJÍ: Long time, e e h? Oh those were fantastic days at Jakute University. Remember 'The Bug', 'The Scorpion', 'The Bleach', etc, etc.

LÁSÚN: Yes those magazines you guys were fond of using to witchhunt women ... especially those of you who never quite succeeded with them.

DÉRẸMÍ: And the Kyrates whose midnight songs made you wet your bed.

DÉRẸMÍ: Yes, and the Purites who nurtured the campus aristocracy and went about in pin-stripe suits like opulent diplomats. *(They laugh)*

TÚNJÍ: Remember what happened when one of them took Obi's girlfriend?

DÉRẸMÍ: He promised to slap him in Richard Hall, knowing full well that our gentleman would only turn the other cheek, for doing that is all that is pure. *(They all laugh)*

LÁSÚN: And that Beast of No Nation who embezzled Student Union funds...
TÚNJÍ: But later told the auditors that he lost one thousand pounds while prostrating for an uncle at Heathrow Airport during a student conference in London. *(After a brief pause)*
LÁSÚN: But folks, jokes apart, tell me, what's this you're wearing? You look like Captain Newton making a case in the British parliament for the legitimacy of the slave trade.
DÉRẸMÍ: Not that we like this, but it's the order of the day.
LÁSÚN: What order? What day?
DÉRẸMÍ: You know whose daughter I am marrying. You have very little say before rich people.
LÁSÚN: You worked yourself into this, old boy. You compromised your freedom.
TÚNJÍ: I told him so.
LÁSÚN: That's right, but you too are in the same outlandish costume.
TÚNJÍ: Yes, I did that to please him.
LÁSÚN: Please, please, please. Must we not displease on principle? If we all lie with our necks to the same side because we are all afraid of displeasing, or being different, it will take only ọnẹ knife to slit all our throats. We criticise our society but frequently take part in those ills we so tirelessly chastise. We lambast emergency millionaires but frantically

	run after their daughters so that we can share in their wealth, the wealth which we know is amassed through oppression; the wealth which we know creates poverty for the majority of our people.
TÚNJÍ:	But one thing ...
LÁSÚN:	No 'but, but' folks. I think it is time to stop chasing with the hounds and running with the hares—all at the same time *(Pause, in a very pensive mood)*. What happened to the dreams we had, the dreams we nursed together as students at the university? I remember that we looked all around our society and what we saw were the monsters of greed and graft, of inefficiency, of lack of consideration for others, of the deification of money and property. We decided to be different. It was a solemn pledge to let the world know there is a healthy alternative, that ours was not a society irredeemably bound to ruin. What happened? Are these bow ties and tail-coats part of those dreams? Is this desperate bid to be son-in-law to a filthy millionaire part of that dream?
DÉRÈMÍ:	You have spoken well, Lásún. But there are crucial problems in adulthood which frustrate the dreams of adolescence. You know I would have married Tòyín. I loved her. She was brilliant and charming, and so on. But I

sat down and thought about the whole matter. Like me, Toyin is the daughter of very poor parents with a train of brothers and sisters to support and educate. Add her six brothers and sisters to my own eight and imagine what problems we would have had in our hands. Remember we would have our own kids. So I thought, to break the poverty cycle, it would be better to marry somebody with greater means, and whom I also love.

LÁSÚN: Only goodness knows whether that will break what you call 'the poverty cycle.' But one thing is certain: there's no way you can share in that wealth without losing your ideals. In fact, from the way you look and talk, you are already a tainted man.

TÚNJÍ: I think your fears are genuine, Lásún. We bend our resolves once in a while, but I think some kinds of compromise are a recipe for death and betrayal. A sure way to self-destruction.

LÁSÚN: We said this times without number when we were students - that you can't choose to be different in our present society without a cost, without suffering in many, many ways. The life of a non-conformist is one of **harrowing loneliness even in the midst of a** chorusing crowd. It is a life exposed to blackmail, to persecution, to calumny of all sorts. You are always being watched, your every slip magnified into a huge blunder to discredit you and justify the status quo. It has always been like that. But you must take care not to stumble, especially when you know there is none around to help you stand; only those too ready to suppress you and still your voice. I know how easy it is to get frustrated. I too have had my own bouts of frustration. But I am irrevocably resolved not to despair. The system will not rejoice over the demise of my dream.

(A loud music explodes off stage. Within an instant about six young women dance on-stage followed by a group of drummers, singing:

Dérẹmí o	*Dérẹmí o*
Ọmọ Ọlọ́lá	Child of the wealthy
Dérẹmí o	*Dérẹmí o*
Ọmọ ọlọ́lá	Child of the prosperous
Dérẹmí o	*Dérẹmí o*
Ọmọ olówó	Child of the rich
Dérẹmí o	*Dérẹmí o*
Ọmọ Ọlọ́rọ̀	Child of the well-to-do.

(The women spread their head-ties on the ground for Dérẹmí to walk on. He sombrely throws one or two notes on the head-ties. There is an accentuation of the drumming, dancing, and singing as the performers file off stage).

TÚNJÍ: Do you believe that?

DÉRẸ́MÍ: *(Sarcastically)* Of course, I do. Isn't it obvious? *(They all laugh)* I'm sure my parents must also be laughing where they are.

LÁSÚN:	Well, the praise-singer's voice is made of sugar. *(Pause)* I don't mean to sadden you on your happy day, Dérẹ̀mí, but we must realize that we live in hard times. The forces of reaction of those who think that the world is for them to dominate and pillage are devising new strategies daily. They dangle their ill-gotten wealth before us. Some of our former comrades have crossed to the other side. They are now being paraded as signs of the failure of the ideal which we cherish and expouse. But we have enough on our side to convince the world that positive revolution is not an empty talk. We shall surely show that our vision of tomorrow is not an adolescent fad.
TÚNJÍ:	Those are fine words, Lásún. We are happy you're still as steadfast as the sun on a cloudless day. *(Turning to Dérẹ̀mí, who is lost in thought).* I think we need occasional doses of this kind of tonic against reactionary conformism which keeps beckoning you to come over to join in, to fall in line. The pressure is so extensive, so overwhelming, but victory begins in not succumbing.

(Another set of singers and dancers bursts in, accompanied by drummers. They dance. Exit).

Black Out.

IV

(Same day; morning still. Chief Chamberlain's sitting room. A large wedding crowd all dressed to kill, getting ready to leave for the church. A flurry of activities. Chamberlain emerges from one of the rooms resplendent in expensive 'agbada', a thick gold necklace with a cross pendant, and rows and rows of red-bead necklaces. His entry is marked by an outburst of singing and dancing. One of the singers raises his praise-name, its chorus spreads like wildfire through the crowd. Chamberlain brings out a wad of crisp currency notes and scatters it among the crowd. Loud approbation. He joins the dancing, with measured steps at first, becoming more involved as the merriment progresses. Then, all of a sudden, two uniformed men burst in through the front door. The merriment stops abruptly. One of the men walks briskly towards Chamberlain, speaking with studied courtesy)

CUSTOM OFFICER: You must be Chief Chamberlain, Sir?

CHIEF CHAMBERLAIN: Yes, and what has that got to do with this rude interruption of a celebration in my own house?

(Whispers from the crowd who has now withdrawn to the background)

CUSTOM OFFICER: I'm sorry, Sir, but I have orders to effect your arrest.

(Exclamation from the crowd)

CHIEF CHAMBERLAIN: *(Shocked)* A a r r e ... s t?
When did weddings become a criminal offence in this country?
(Wedding bells start ringing in the background)
CUSTOM OFFICER: Not the wedding Sir, but the car.
CHIEF CHAMBERLAIN: And what about the car? Is it no longer lawful for me to get my daughter to the church in the car of my choice?
CUSTOM OFFICER: The car, Sir, the one parked in front...
CHIEF CHAMBERLAIN: Yes, what about the car? See man, that car is the centre of today's wedding and...
CUSTOM OFFICER: I know, Sir, I also suspect that the car was smuggled into the country. The ports have no evidence of its importation.
CHIEF CHAMBERLAIN: Who sent you on this silly errand? If you were asked to deliver a message as a slave, why haven't you decided to do so as a freeborn?
CUSTOM OFFICER: *(Bringing a piece of paper from his pocket).* This long talk is useless, Sir. Here's your warrant of arrest.
(Exclamation from the crowd)
CHIEF CHAMBERLAIN: Tuck that stupid thing back in your even more stupid pocket. Go away. I'll take this matter up from above. Today is the happiest day of my life, and no uniformed scoundrel is going to ruin it for me.
(Wedding bells are ringing in the background)

CUSTOM OFFICER: My own order came from above, Sir. Otherwise I wouldn't be here.
(The crowd is becoming restless. Some of them are already sneaking away)
CHIEF CHAMBERLAIN: Oh I see! The water dragon does not dance for nothing: its drummers are inside the water. The general election is around the corner. *(Now musing to himself)*. But why have my enemies decided to take their pound of flesh on my happiest day? And with all the fortune I gave to those rogues at the ports. Or didn't your bosses tell you that I have already seen them? Didn't they give you your own share?
CUSTOM OFFICER: I ...
CHIEF CHAMBERLAIN: Ok, tell your masters I will see them again after the wedding. Tell the...
CUSTOM OFFICER: I have orders for immediate arrest, Sir.
(Wedding bells are ringing in the background)
CHIEF CHAMBERLAIN: *(becoming importunate)* Ok... and you... you need something to make that lean waistline a little rounder... what do you want? How much ...?
CUSTOM OFFICER: Sir, I hope you don't intend to add 'obstruction of justice,' or, 'resistance of arrest,' to your list of offences ...?
(Most of the crowd has now left, with only a handful remaining)
You are to come with me, Sir. And the car is hereby impounded.

(Chief Chamberlain, sensing that the game is up, rises, deflated, from his chair, and walks like a ghost across the stage. He staggers off stage, the custom officers following.
Slow light out, the wedding bells still ringing in the background).

GLOSSARY

The Man Who Walked Away

p.2   *Udoji* severe inflation (named after Chief Jerome Udoji, chairman of a wage review panel in the 70's, the wrongful implementaton of whose recommendations led to excessive wage increases and inflation).

p.2   *bósíkónà* second-hand clothes.

p.4   *ọ̀gá pátápátá* big boss

p.7   *Olówóoríimi* the-one-who-owns-me; my lord.

p.8   *ṣọ́rọ́* trousers (indigenous Yoruba dress)

p.8   *dànṣíkí* top garment (indigenous Yoruba dress)

p.9   *ṣekẹndí alùwọnjọn wọnjọn lapo ṣoju ọmọ rèjerèje* the stuff; the one that jingles in the pocket and gives its rich owner a smooth face.

p.14   *ayò* an indigenous game played in leisure time

p.16   *jábúrẹ́dì* an expensive cloth of the velvet type

p.17   *gèlè* head gear; *iborùn*: shawl draped across the shoulders by women

p.19   *Baba o* Big boss; *àjẹpẹ́ ayé!* long life!

p.20   *O tooo* Enough! Silence!

p.20   *K'ójú máá ríbí, ẹsẹ̀ loogun ẹ* That the eyes may not see evil, the legs must be alert.

p.20   *gbogbo ara loògun è* the whole body must be alert.

p.21   *Saara* charity donation; sacrifice

p.26   *Òkú Èkó* Lagos corpse, a derisive name for frozen fish

p.26   *Ó-ṣè-wọ* concessional

The Wedding Car

p.32 *asòpá* one with swollen testicles or elephantiasis of the scrotum.

p.34 *bùbá* top garment usually with wide sleeves

p.34 *agbádá* flowing garment usually worn by men.

p.34 *Ọbọkuń Bàbá! Mẹesi Ọlóyè oníbèbè pombé! Kọ́róbọ́tọ́ bí oká* The great glossy one! Unmatchable Mercedes, which boasts a swathe of beads! Plump like a cobra

p.34 *ankara* a cotton fabric with rich colours

p.34 *aṣọ ẹbí* uniform attire worn by celebrants.

p.40 *Ó tóóó.* Enough, silence!

p.47 *Adú-má-ra dán, oníbàdíòréke.* One-whose-black-ness-enhances-her body, one with firm attractive buttocks.

p.48 *Ògún* is the Yoruba god of iron.

p.50 *Ìbàdíàrań, ọmọ ajífọláwẹ ọmọ ajífowoṣanwọ́.* Precious one, one-who-bathes-in-wealth, one-who-washes-her-hands-with-money.

p.51 *Iyán, àmàlà, ẹkọ, móínmóín* are different Nigerian foods

p.53 *Baba, kẹ́ẹ gbo, kẹ́ẹ tọ́ọ́* Papa, may you live long

p.53 *Ire a kárí o* May good things go round to all

p.57 *Ó le jùù!* This is just superb!

p.58 *Ọbọkuń* A kind of expensive fish relished as a delicacy in Nigeria.

p.58 *Oyinbo pọ̀!* Too much English!